IT'S THE END OF THE WORLD!

NUCLEAR WAR

BY ALLAN MOREY

BELLWETHER MEDIA • MINNEAPOLIS, MN

TM

Are you ready to take it to the extreme? Torque books thrust you into the action-packed world of sports, vehicles, mystery, and adventure. These books may include dirt, smoke, fire, and chilling tales. **WARNING**: read at your own risk.

This edition first published in 2020 by Bellwether Media, Inc.

No part of this publication may be reproduced in whole or in part without written permission of the publisher.
For information regarding permission, write to Bellwether Media, Inc.,
Attention: Permissions Department,
6012 Blue Circle Drive, Minnetonka, MN 55343.

Library of Congress Cataloging-in-Publication Data

Names: Morey, Allan, author.
Title: Nuclear War / By Allan Morey.
Description: Minneapolis, MN : Bellwether Media, Inc., 2020. |
    Series: Torque: It's the End of the World! | Includes bibliographical
    references and index. | Audience: Age 7-12.
Identifiers: LCCN 2019000973 (print) | LCCN 2019004507 (ebook) |
    ISBN 9781618916532 (ebook) | ISBN 9781644870822
    (hardcover : alk. paper)
Subjects: LCSH: Nuclear warfare–Juvenile literature.
Classification: LCC U263 (ebook) | LCC U263 .M667 2020 (print) |
    DDC 355.02/17–dc23
LC record available at https://lccn.loc.gov/2019000973

Editor: Rebecca Sabelko   Designer: Andrea Schneider

Printed in the United States of America, North Mankato, MN.

TABLE OF CONTENTS

MUSHROOM CLOUD!

You have been watching the news for weeks. North Korean troops gather on the border with South Korea. The United States is sending forces to stop an **invasion**.

Then warnings sound. North Korea has launched a nuclear **missile**!

A WAR WITH NO WINNER

The Korean War ended with no winner. Conflict continues between North and South Korea.

...G NEWS

...A HAS LAUNCHED A NUCLEAR MISSILE

...S ADVISED TO SEEK IMMEDIATE SHELTER

...THE UNITED STATES ARMED FORCES, A NUCLEAR MISSILE IS SAID TO HA...

ILLUSTRATION OF A MUSHROOM CLOUD

You rush to a bomb shelter. An explosion rocks the area. A mushroom cloud rises from the blast.

A **blast wave** expands from the explosion. Buildings are flattened. Fires start. You wonder what will be left of the world outside.

THE BIG NINE

Nine countries have nuclear weapons. The U.S. and Russia have the most. France and the United Kingdom have many as well. Other countries include China, India, Pakistan, Israel, and North Korea.

A BOMB IS DROPPED

Nuclear bombs are the strongest weapons on Earth. Just one can destroy everything for miles around. But many bombs would be used in a nuclear war.

A bomb's **detonation** begins with a bright flash. The flash warns people seconds before the blast wave hits. Miles of land are flattened. Fires blaze. Deadly **radiation** spreads far beyond the **blast zone**.

DETONATION

KA-BOOM!

The strength of nuclear bombs is measured in kilotons.
One kiloton is equal to 1,000 tons of TNT!

**PLANES DROPPING BOMBS
IN WORLD WAR II**

Bombs continue to fall from the sky.
Flattened cities dot the landscape.
Radiation destroys many of the living
things left behind.

Ash from the bombs blocks out the
sun. Temperatures drop. The planet
goes into a nuclear winter. Those who
remain alive struggle to survive.

Governments have plans to keep their leaders safe in a nuclear war. Leaders head to **bunkers**. These rooms can withstand most nuclear blasts.

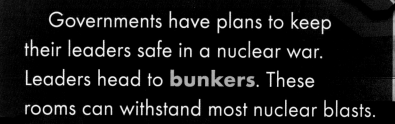

BUNKER

Everyone else gathers supplies. They seek out shelter and stay indoors. Being inside can protect against radiation.

CHAIN REACTION

conflict between countries rise and war begins

as the war goes on, nuclear missiles are launched

nuclear blasts and radiation affect millions of people

the world goes into a nuclear winter as ash blocks out the sun

most plants and animals do not survive the temperature drop

THE INTRODUCTION OF NUCLEAR WAR

Nuclear war became a reality on August 6, 1945. The U.S. wanted to end its **conflict** with Japan. The U.S. sent the *Enola Gay* to drop Little Boy on Hiroshima. Little Boy was the first nuclear bomb used in war. Japan **surrendered** soon after.

FAT MAN BLAST

A LOOK BACK:
THE ATOM BOMBS

AUGUST 6 AND 9, 1945

HIROSHIMA AND NAGASAKI, JAPAN

Little Boy and Fat Man destroyed the cities of Hiroshima and Nagasaki. The effects of the bombs continued to affect people for decades after.

B-29 BOMBER *ENOLA GAY*

U.S. NAVY

U.S. NAVY LEADING SOVIET SHIP AWAY FROM CUBA

SOVIET SHIP

SOVIET MISSILE FROM CUBAN MISSILE CRISIS

Nuclear war became a threat again in 1962. It began when the **Soviets** moved nuclear missiles to Cuba. The U.S. set up a **blockade** of the island. The conflict became known as the Cuban Missile Crisis. It ended when the Soviets removed the weapons.

WILL NUCLEAR WAR HAPPEN AGAIN?

World War II made nuclear war a reality. It showed how destructive nuclear weapons can be. No one has used a nuclear bomb since.

But conflicts have continued in recent years between nuclear powers. North Korea and the United States have had disagreements. India and Pakistan have gone to war over territory.

IN THE MEDIA

BOOK TITLE: *BOMB: THE RACE TO BUILD — AND STEAL — THE WORLD'S MOST DANGEROUS WEAPON*

AUTHOR: STEVE SHEINKIN

YEAR RELEASED: 2012

Bomb is the true story about the creation of the atomic bomb. Sheinkin uses the lives of scientists, spies, and others to explain the race for atomic science.

NUCLEAR STOCKPILE

There are about 15,000 nuclear weapons in the world.

The **Nuclear Non-Proliferation Treaty** was created in 1968. It stopped the spread of nuclear weapons. It also states countries cannot develop and test nuclear weapons. Nuclear war will not be part of our future as long as countries follow this treaty.

GLOSSARY

blast wave—the heat and pressure from a nuclear bomb that moves out from the initial blast

blast zone—the area of land that is affected by the blast wave of a nuclear explosion

blockade—an act of war in which one country uses troops or ships to stop people or supplies from entering or leaving another country

bunkers—strong underground shelters

conflict—a disagreement over power

detonation—the action of an explosion

invasion—when the military from one country moves into another country

missile—a weapon that flies through the air to strike a distant target

Nuclear Non-Proliferation Treaty—an agreement made by countries that says they will not test or make new nuclear weapons and they will disarm current nuclear weapons

radiation—a type of dangerous and powerful energy that is released by a nuclear bomb

Soviets—the people, especially the political and military leaders, of the former Soviet Union; the Soviet Union was a group of countries in Eastern Europe and Northern Asia from 1922 to 1991.

surrendered—agreed to stop fighting

TO LEARN MORE

AT THE LIBRARY

Hudak, Heather. *Nuclear Weapons and the Arms Race*. New York, N.Y.: Crabtree Publishing, 2018.

McCoy, Erin L. *Nuclear Confrontation*. New York, N.Y.: Cavendish Square, 2019.

Smibert, Angie. *12 Incredible Facts about the Dropping of the Atomic Bombs*. North Mankato, Minn.: 12-Story Library, 2016.

ON THE WEB

FACTSURFER

Factsurfer.com gives you a safe, fun way to find more information.
1. Go to www.factsurfer.com
2. Enter "nuclear war" into the search box and click 🔍.
3. Select your book cover to see a list of related web sites.

INDEX

The images in this book are reproduced through the courtesy of: Sean Pavone, front cover (city before); solarseven, front cover, pp. 2-3, 20-21 (mushroom cloud); IgorZh, front cover, pp. 2-3, 20-21 (city after); Andrey_Popov, pp. 4-5 (couple); Yeongsik Im, pp. 4-5 (TV screen); mwreck, pp. 6-7 (city); KREML, pp. 6-7 (mushroom cloud); Stocktrek Images, Inc./ Alamy, pp. 8-9; SugaBom86, pp. 10-11; Everett Historical, p. 11 (planes inset); Boris Rabtsevich, pp. 12-13; Gorodenkoff, p. 13 (top left); Alexyz3d, p. 13 (top right); Jina K, p. 13 (middle left); G Tipene, p. 13 (middle right); EhayDy, p. 13 (bottom middle); Veinsworld/ Wiki Commons, pp. 14-15 (plane); Charles Levey/ Wikipedia, p. 15 (Fat Man blast); Everett Collection Inc/ Alamy, pp. 16-17; Vadim Nefedoff, p. 17 (missile inset); Wiki Commons, pp. 18-19; Wikipedia, p. 19 (Bomb cover); Rena Schild, p. 21 (protest inset).